Around the World
in Eighty Poems

Around the World in Eighty Poems

Compiled by
Jennifer and Graeme Curry

Illustrated by Mark Southgate

Hutchinson
London Melbourne Auckland Johannesburg

For TYM, with love and laughter

First published in 1988 by Hutchinson Children's Books
An imprint of Century Hutchinson Ltd
Brookmount House, 62–65 Chandos Place,
Covent Garden London WC2N 4NW

Century Hutchinson Australia Pty Ltd
16–22 Church Street, Hawthorn, Melbourne,
Victoria 3122

Century Hutchinson New Zealand Limited
32–34 View Road, PO Box 40-086, Glenfield,
Auckland 10

Century Hutchinson South Africa (Pty) Ltd
PO Box 337, Bergvlei 2012, South Africa

Set in Garamond by BookEns, Saffron Walden, Essex

Printed and bound in Great Britain by
Anchor Brendon Ltd, Tiptree, Essex

British Library Cataloguing in Publication Data
Around the world in eighty poems.
1. English poetry
I. Curry, Jennifer   II. Curry, Graeme
821'.008'09282   PR1175.3

ISBN 0-09-172190-3

Contents

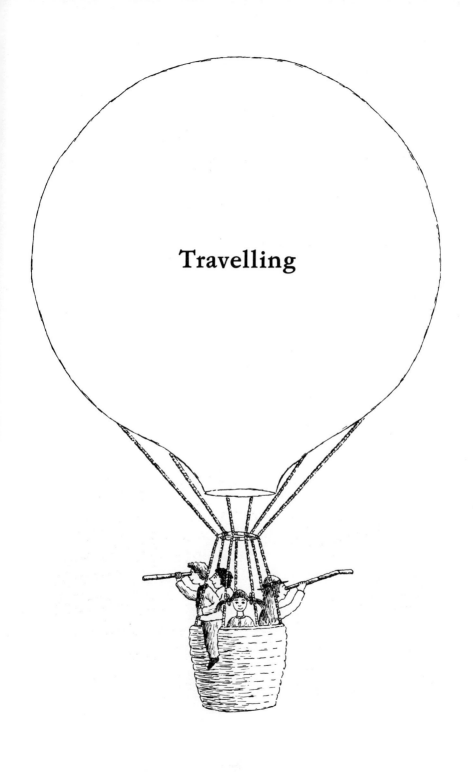

Travelling

The traveller

The world is vast in the light of my torch
  As I travel it all in secret
From Pole to Pole, to where East becomes West,
  Curled up in the tent of my blanket.

My finger pressed to the map, I visit
  Lands where hardly anything grows;
And mountain, mesa, plain or plateau
  Where the milk and the honey flows.

With me as the Captain, stern at the wheel,
  Over always-blue seas I follow
The course of the S.S. Aurora
  From Bremen to Val Paraiso.

I cross the green countries, the pink and the brown –
  In Madagascar I settle
To see the indris swing in the trees, then – leap!
  To Popocatepetl!

I plunge into thick dark rain-forests
  Of the Congo or Nigeria,
And come back again to the world of men
  Driving a train in Siberia.

Now I sign on for a spell of cow-punching
  In the state of Saskatchewan,
Now I dance on the grapes in Hungary
  And they play me a gipsy tune.

Then over the blazing Sahara I tramp
  To Fez, thirsty, weary'n'sore –
Then I share succotash with the little girl
  From Little Rock, Arkansas.

I drop into Khartoum, where I change to the plane
  That takes me to Samarkand;
I sunbathe a day – and then, I'm away,
  To a slalom, in Switzerland.

In Rio I play football with Pele
  And beat England, at Maracana,
Buy a huge sack of coffee, for a good brew-up
  By the Wabash, in Indiana.

In Lapland the reindeer are browsing
  By the light of the midnight sun;
While Indians still sleep in the Andes,
  And in Nassau are Yanks, having fun.

But in Tibet I felt suddenly homesick,
  Lonely, and a little bit sad –
So I switched off my torch and came out
  Back into my room, in my bed.

Brian Lee

A trip to Morrow

I started on a journey just about a week ago
For the little town of Morrow in the State of Ohio.
I never was a traveller and really didn't know
That Morrow had been ridiculed a century or so.
I went down to the depot for my ticket and applied
For tips regarding Morrow, interviewed the station
    guide.
Said I, 'My friend, I want to go to Morrow and
    return
Not later than tomorrow, for I haven't time to
    burn.'

Said he to me, 'Now let me see, if I have heard you
    right,
You want to go to Morrow and come back
    tomorrow night,
You should have gone to Morrow yesterday and
    back today,
For if you started yesterday to Morrow, don't you
    see
You should have got to Morrow and returned
    today at three.
The train that started yesterday, now understand
    me right,
Today it gets to Morrow and returns tomorrow
    night.'

'Now if you start to Morrow, you will surely land
Tomorrow into Morrow, not today you understand,
For the train today to Morrow, if the schedule is
    right
Will get you into Morrow by about tomorrow
    night.'
Said I, 'I guess you know it all, but kindly let me
    say,
How can I go to Morrow if I leave the town today?'

Said he, 'You cannot go to Morrow any more
      today,
For the train that goes to Morrow is a mile upon
      its way.'

Anon

The last steam train to Margate

Gossssh
I wisssh
I were a busss
It's muccch less work
And muccch less fuss
I ssshould like that
I ssschould like that
I SSSSCHOULD like that
I ssshould like that
De-deedle-dee
De-diddle-dum
Just look at me
'Cause here I come
Faster and faster
Tickerty-boo, what'll I do?
Tearing along, terribly fast
Singing a song, sounding a blast
Whoo, whoo! Out of the way
Goodness me, I can't delay!
You can relax, I have to run
Follow the tracks into the sun
Pain in my back, aches in my joints
Tickerty-tack, here are the points
Diddly-dee, diddly dee
Diddly WIDDLY diddly dee!
Far to go? Not very far.
Little black tunnel
(Tickerty WHAAAH!)
Look over there. What can it be?
Lucky old you, clever old me
Come all this way, never go wrong,
Come every day, singing a song
Down to the seaside. Let's have a cheer.
Oh, what a train-ride. We're nearly there,
We're nearly there, we're nearly there, we're nearly
    there

And now I'd better slow right down
In half a mile we reach the town
And then you take your buckets and spades
And dig the sand and watch the parades
And sing and paddle and splash in the sea
And have ice cream and jelly for tea
And Coca Cola, orange squassssh
And ginger beer, hooray we're here
But gosssh I'm tired
Oh gosssh I'm tired
Oh gosssh I'm tired
Hohhh
GOSSSSSSSSSSSSSSHHHHHHHHHHHHHH

John Hill

Night train to Istanbul

Some whispered tales which I have heard
Although I know they're quite absurd,
Say strange things happen on this train,
Things the Turks can't quite explain.
  Through the night to Istanbul,
  Roaring, rushing, through the night.

You lose your passport, or your life,
Your wallet and perhaps your wife;
Folks disappear, and blinds are drawn
Before the border and the dawn.
  Through the night to Istanbul,
  Rocking, rolling, through the night.

Deals in diamonds, deadly drugs,
Lovely women, crooks, and thugs,
Coded plans and cold-eyed killers,
The kind of thing you meet in thrillers.
  Through the night to Istanbul,
  Rattling, raging, through the night.

I think that blonde might be a spy,
I cannot look her in the eye;
The slant-eyed man could be a crook;
The train attendant has that look.
  Through the night to Istanbul,
  Whistling, wailing, through the night.

I think they stretch a point or two,
I hardly think it can be true;
But if I'm killed I shall complain,
And never use this train again.
  Through the night to Istanbul,
  Rooting, tooting, through the night.

A. Elliott-Cannon

The fastest train in the world

Tokyo to Kyoto
 tokyotokyoto
kyotokyotokyotokyo
 tokyotokyoto

Keith Bosley

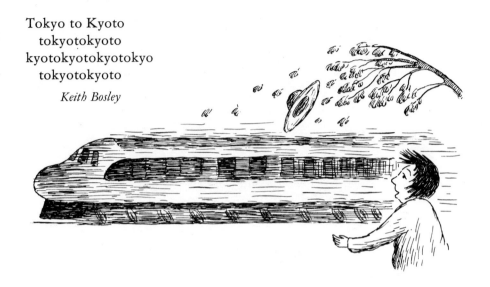

Crossing Ireland by train

The evening light is longer here.
It romps across the greenest fields
and turns black bushes into runners.
No one watches.

The empty lake belongs to sunsets
with a single sail stuck on it.
Close by the shore a ruined tower
talks to itself in whispers.

Kings and queens were buried here
in these round hills
with stones above them.
Their shadows race across their kingdoms.

Jane Whittle

Victoria

From Victoria I can go
To Pevensey Level and Piddinghoe,
Open Winkins and Didling Hill,
Three Cups Corner and Selsey Bill.
I'm the happiest one in all the nation
When my train runs out of Victoria Station.

But O the day when I come to town
From Ditchling Beacon and Duncton Down,
Bramber Castle and Wisborough Green,
Cissbury Ring and Ovingdean!
I'm the sorriest one in all the nation
When my train runs into Victoria Station.

Eleanor Farjeon

Adlestrop

Yes. I remember Adlestrop –
The name, because one afternoon
Of heat the express-train drew up there
Unwontedly. It was late June.

The steam hissed. Some one cleared his throat.
No one left and no one came
On the bare platform. What I saw
Was Adlestrop – only the name

And willows, willow-herb, and grass,
And meadowsweet, and haycocks dry,
No whit less still and lonely fair
Than the high cloudlets in the sky.

And for that minute a blackbird sang
Close by, and round him, mistier,
Farther and farther, all the birds
Of Oxfordshire and Gloucestershire.

Edward Thomas

17

The subway in New York

Here forests of skyscrapers
Compete with one another in height
Among the splendour and grandeur
Which this mammoth city prides in.
I found, however, its subway quite miserable.
The window-frames of the car I got into
Were encrusted with much rust.
Its matted seats were worn
And torn and disembowelled.
Dirty were the window-panes,
Spoiled with many rain-marks,
Through which I could see only dimly
The shifting scenes of the outside world,
When the car came out of the long, noisy tube.
Quite disappointed, I stole a glance
At the magazine a girl was reading
And found she was poring over
The recent fashions in Paris.

Tsutoma Fukuda

18

Cargoes

Quinquireme of Nineveh from distant Ophir,
Rowing home to haven in sunny Palestine,
With a cargo of ivory,
And apes and peacocks,
Sandalwood, cedarwood, and sweet white wine.

Stately Spanish galleon coming from the Isthmus,
Dipping through the Tropics by the palm-green
    shores,
With a cargo of diamonds,
Emeralds, amethysts,
Topazes, and cinnamon, and gold moidores.

Dirty British coaster with a salt-caked smoke stack
Butting through the Channel in the mad March
    days,
With a cargo of Tyne coal,
Road-rail, pig-lead,
Firewood, ironware, and cheap tin trays.

John Masefield

Bangor boat

Bangor boat's away!
We have no time to stay.
One in a boat
Two in a boat
Bangor boat's away.

Playground rhyme

19

At Kisagata

At Kisagata
A cherry tree is covered
At times by the waves:
Fishermen must row their boats
Above the cherry blossoms.

Matsuo Basho
(Seventeenth century Japanese)

Beginning of the Armadilloes

I've never sailed the Amazon,
  I've never reached Brazil;
But the Don and Magalena,
  They can go there when they will!

        Yes, weekly from Southampton,
        Great steamers, white and gold,
          Go rolling down to Rio
        (Roll down – roll down to Rio!)
          And I'd like to roll to Rio
        Some day before I'm old!

I've never seen a Jaguar,
  Nor yet an Armadill –
O dilloing in his armour,
  And I s'pose I never will,

          Unless I go to Rio
        These wonders to behold –
       Roll down – roll down to Rio –
         Roll really down to Rio!
        Oh, I'd love to roll to Rio
        Some day before I'm old!

Rudyard Kipling

Travel

I should like to rise and go
Where the golden apples grow;
Where below another sky
Parrot islands anchored lie,
And, watched by cockatoos and goats,
Lonely Crusoes building boats;
Where in sunshine reaching out
Eastern cities, miles about,
Are with mosque and minaret
Among sandy gardens set,
And the rich goods from near and far
Hang for sale in the bazaar;
Where the Great Wall round China goes,
And on one side the desert blows,
And with bell and voice and drum,
Cities on the other hum;
Where are forests, hot as fire,
Wide as England, tall as a spire,
Full of apes and cocoa-nuts
And the negro hunters' huts;
Where the knotty crocodile
Lies and blinks in the Nile,
And the red flamingo flies
Hunting fish before his eyes;
Where in jungles, near and far,
Man-devouring tigers are,
Lying close and giving ear
Lest the hunt be drawing near,
Or a comer-by be seen
Swinging in a palanquin;
Where among the desert sands
Some deserted city stands,
All its children, sweep and prince,
Grown to manhood ages since,
Not a foot in street or house,
Not a stir of child or mouse,

And when kindly falls the night,
In all the town no spark of light.
There I'll come when I'm a man
With a camel caravan;
Light a fire in the gloom
Of some dusty dining-room;
See the pictures on the walls,
Heroes, fights and festivals;
And in a corner find the toys
Of the old Egyptian boys.

R. L. Stevenson

21

France at a glance:
a holiday in a hurry

This is the way to holiday –
M25, M2
Over 70 all the way
The radio and you.

Over the Channel the quickest way
(By Hovercraft) we'll tear
Then fast as we can through Normandy
To beat the traffic there.

Let's hurry on to Paris, Harry
And then I fancy Nancy
But let's not stay in the North all day
If the weather there is chancy.

We'll motor on to Besançon
Or buzz across to Basel –
Or perhaps Dijon – Chalon – Lyon?
That looks less of a hassle.

It's lovely in Lausanne, you say?
And over the Haute Savoie?
Yes, I know you're fond of Switzerland
But think of the strain on the car.

It's up and down and round and round
And terribly bad for the brakes:
I say we take the motorway
To Avignon or Aix.

Well, here we are; we've come ever so far
And it's much too dark to see
But tomorrow we'll go to Monaco
Or Spain or Italy.

Will you pop and post the postcards?
I've written them in advance:
'Wish you were here, etcetera –
   Not much to see in France.'

Ian Whybrow

Babylon

How many miles to Babylon?
   Three score miles and ten.
Can I get there by candle-light?
   Yes, and back again.

Anon

Rickshaw ride

That man by the harbour
Spitting into the water
Is as old as China.

He is made of leather
And his folded face
Is like a sandbar
At low tide.
Will you take a ride
On his rickshaw?

He will not thank you
For your dollar
He knows that to you
A dollar does not matter.
Off you go with a clatter
Up to Victoria
On up the long hill
Past the cathedral
To the Peak Tram.

Pull! Pull!
He leans to it.
His muscles at neck and calf and shoulder
And his dark veins that snake
Take your eye
Not what passes by.
Let him not break
Something for my sake,
For my dollar.

You went to Hong Kong
They will say.
Did you take a rickshaw?
Was it fun?
Did he run, your rickshaw man?

Yes, he ran.
No, it was not much fun.

John Hill

24

How a car-journey to the Black Forest made a liar out of an honest woman

Mum, what are we going camping for?
   Because it's so much fun.
But will it rain like it did last year?
   This year there'll be sun.

Mum, is it far to Germany?
   Not now that we're in France.
Can we stop for a cup of tea?
   When we get the chance.

Mum, can we stop *now*? I feel ill.
This rucksack's squashing me.
   You'll feel much better if you sit still.
   Try it and you'll see.

Mum, can we have the music up?
   The music is up now.
But can't we have it louder?
   That's as loud as it will go.

Mum, John has pinched me hard
And my arms are going black!
   If you two don't behave yourselves
   We'll turn round and go back.

Oh look, mum, there's a Pizza Hut!
   What a shame, I think it's shut.

Mum, is it far to Strasbourg now?
   Not very far!
And is Wildberg much further?
   We'll be there in about an hour.

Mum, do you know something? – No, I don't.
  Whatever is it now?
You've just told twelve lies in a row
And we've *still* got miles to go.

Ian Whybrow

A post card from Greece

The sun over here makes us browner,
after the burning wears off;
this blue kind of water is warmer
and waves are never as rough.

The flowers that grow here are brighter,
we stay up much later, to eat;
white painted houses are whiter,
the coffee is thicker, and sweet.

With sand in my undies,
cheese in the salad
and a hole in the bathroom floor,

with beds that feel harder
and days that seem longer
with things to be looking for

like donkeys and tortoises,
cats and cooked octopuses
and wine in the water to drink,

with castles on mountains
and thousands of candles
I like it in Greece, I think.

Jane Whittle

Fun and fantasy

Ball-bouncing game

Long-legged Italy
Kicked poor Sicily
Into the middle of the Mediterranean Sea.
Austria was Hungary,
Took a bit of Turkey,
Dipped it in Greece,
Fried it in Japan,
And ate it off China.

Traditional

The sleeptrotting globewisher

I wish I lived in Holland
Where they don't have hills and valleys:
I'd make Dutch cheese with finger-holes
And have lots of bowling-alleys.

Or perhaps in Gorgonzola Land
Where the cheese is very smelly,
I'd invent a cheese-deodorant
And get myself on telly.

I wish I lived in Canada
Where the syrup grows on trees:
I'd breed some Breadandbutterflies
And pension off the bees.

If I were a New Zealander
Where the Kiwis run around,
I'd fit them all with rotor-blades
To get them off the ground.

I wish I lived in Norway
Where the arctic winds criss-cross:
I'd fill my mouth with sugar-lumps
And breathe out candy-floss.

And I wish I lived in Sweden,
In the land of ice and snow:
I would spit out frozen arrows
And pee a frozen bow.

So many things I'd do with all
These wishes in my head
But I think they might evaporate
If I get out of bed.

Ian Whybrow

29

Three French mice

Three French mice went out for the day –
They went to Paris, but that was too gay.
They went to Bordeaux,
But that was too slow,
They went to Toulouse
And lost their shoes.
They went to Nice
And told the police.
They went to Marseilles
And ate some snails.
But when they got to Spain
They all ran home again.

*Translated from French nursery
rhyme by Rose Fyleman*

Tarragon, tansy, thyme and teasel

Timothy went to Aragon
Riding on a weasel,
To ask the Dons for tarragon,
Tansy, thyme, and teasel.

The Dons they met in Aragon
Didn't like the weasel,
So Timothy got no tarragon,
Tansy, thyme, or teasel.

Eleanor Farjeon

If pigs could fly

If pigs could fly, I'd fly a pig
To foreign countries small and big –
To Italy and Spain,
To Austria, where cowbells ring,
To Germany, where people sing –
And then come home again.

I'd see the Ganges and the Nile;
I'd visit Madagascar's isle,
And Persia and Peru.
People would say they'd never seen
So odd, so strange an air-machine
As that on which I flew.

Why, everyone would raise a shout
To see his trotters and his snout
Come floating from the sky;
And I would be a famous star
Well known in countries near and far –
If only pigs could fly!

James Reeves

The whales off Wales

With walloping tails, the whales off Wales
Whack waves to wicked whitecaps,
And while they snore on their watery floor,
They wear wet woollen nightcaps.

The whales! the whales! the whales of Wales,
They're always spouting fountains,
And as they glide through the tilting tide,
They move like melting mountains.

X. J. Kennedy

31

Australia

Quite obviously in Australia
Everything's upside down;
And you must be an absolute failure
If you happen to wear a crown.

Do you walk, to get through a door,
On the ceiling? Does a bird
Perch out of harm on the floor?
Is 'top' a rather rude word?

Is headball played, and eleveniss?
If you hate anyone is it love?
Of course, they don't know where heaven is
Except that it's not up above.

Are holidays longer than terms?
Are humbugs good for you?
No doubt deep in the sky are worms,
And served first is the last in the queue.

Do dogs sniff each others' noses
And wag them when they are glad?
Are dandelions not roses
Carefully grown by Dad?

Do children go to the office?
Does Mother tell awful lies?
And Grandpa buy comics and toffees,
Gran's skirt give her chilly thighs?

If so, I'll not go to Australia,
Where at jokes a listener sobs.
Besides, I prefer a dahlia
To grow flowers rather than knobs.

Roy Fuller

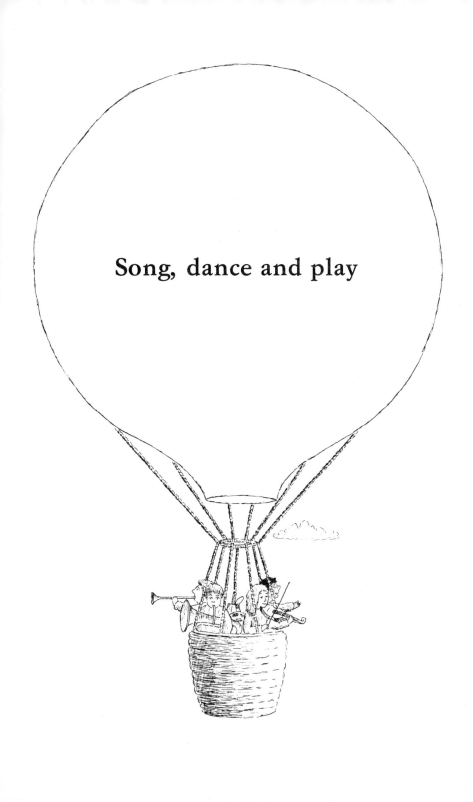

Song, dance and play

Limbo

And limbo stick is the silence in front of me
limbo

limbo
limbo like me
limbo
limbo like me

long dark night is the silence in front of me
limbo
limbo like me
stick hit sound
and the ship like it ready

stick hit sound
and the dark still steady

limbo
limbo like me

long dark deck and the water surrounding me
long dark deck and the silence is over me

limbo
limbo like me
stick is the whip
and the dark deck is slavery

stick is the whip
and the dark deck is slavery

limbo
limbo like me
drum stick knocks
and the darkness is over me

34

knees spread wide
and the water is hiding me

limbo
limbo like me

knees spread wide
and the dark ground is under me

down
down
down

and the drummer is calling me
limbo
limbo like me

sun coming up
and the drummers are praising me

out of the dark
and the dumb gods are raising me

up
up
up
and the music is saving me

hot
slow
step
on the limbo ground

Edward Braithwaite

35

Russian dance

The Russian moujik is made for music,
For music the moujik is most enthusic.
Whenever an instrument twangs or toots
He tucks his trousers into his boots,
He squats on his heels, but his knees don't crack,
And he kicks like a frenzied jumping jack.
My knees would make this performance tragic,
But his have special moujik magic.

Ogden Nash

Note: A moujik is a peasant

May music in Castille

Below in the street, the music began
Of voices, mandolin, accordion, guitar,
That every midnight celebrate the May.
I was in bed, too sleepy by far
Yet again to listen to the minstrels play
Upon sweet mandolin, accordion, guitar,
So my eyelids closed as the melody ran.

But when the music stopped in mid-beat,
Voices and mandolin, accordion, guitar,
And the dumb-struck minstrels went their way,
And in the sky was no summer star
But storm and thunder to see out the May
And the voices, mandolin, accordion, guitar,
I rose for the rain. It strums in the street.

Ted Walker

Singing

The children sing in far Japan,
  The children sing in Spain.
The organ and the organ man
  Are singing in the rain.

R. L. Stevenson

My auntie from Spain

My auntie from Spain had a nasty complaint
Which made her feel dizzy and tired and faint.
She went to the doctor and said, 'Cure me, please!'
He said, 'There's no cure for the waltzing disease!'

As soon as he said it, my aunt lost control
And waltzed herself into a telegraph pole.
The cables came down on my poor auntie's head
And every TV in the country went dead.

She waltzed over people who stood in her way
She waltzed in the bullring and shouted, '*Olé!*'
She waltzed round the bull, as if in a trance,
And graciously showed him the steps of the dance.

The toreador cheered as they waltzed all about,
The matador chortled and almost passed out.
The people joined in till the bullring was full
Of mad waltzing couples, my aunt and the bull.

My auntie got married, I'm happy to say.
The wedding took place on St Valentine's Day.
And if you believe that my tale is untrue
My uncle, the bull, may go waltzing with *you*!

Doug MacLeod

37

The fiddler of Dooney

When I play on my fiddle in Dooney
Folk dance like a wave of the sea;
My cousin is priest in Kilvarnet,
My brother in Mocharabuiee.

I passed my brother and cousin:
They read in their books of prayer;
I read in my book of songs
I bought at the Sligo fair.

When we come at the end of time
To Peter sitting in state,
He will smile on the three old spirits,
But call me first through the gate;

For the good are always the merry,
Save by an evil chance,
And the merry love the fiddle,
And the merry love to dance:

And when the folk there spy me,
They will all come up to me,
With 'Here is the fiddler of Dooney!'
And dance like a wave of the sea.

W. B. Yeats

Chinese Sandmen

Chinese Sandmen,
Wise and creepy,
Croon dream-songs
To make us sleepy.
A Chinese maid with slanting eyes
Is queen of all their lullabies.
On her ancient moon-guitar
She strums a sleep-song to a star;
And when big China-shadows fall
Snow-white lilies hear her call.
Chinese Sandmen,
Wise and creepy,
Croon dream-songs
To make us sleepy.

Anon

Boules

Boules dans le boulevard
A Parisian café
Blue berets and Gauloise smoke
A hazy summer day

Boules dans le boulevard
The river turning grey
Falling leaves and Gauloise smoke
And summer fades away

Benjamin Bolt

The picnic in Jammu

Uncle Ayub swung me round and round
till the horizon became a rail
banked high upon the Himalayas.
The trees signalled me past. I whistled,
shut my eyes through tunnels of the air.
The family laughed, watching me puff
out my muscles, healthily aggressive.

> This was late summer, before the snows
> come to Kashmir, this was picnic time.

Then, uncoupling me from the sky, he
plunged me into the river, himself
a bough with me dangling at its end.
I went purple as a plum. He reared
back and lowered the branch of his arm
to grandma who swallowed me with a kiss.
Laughter peeled away my goosepimples.

> This was late summer, before the snows
> come to Kashmir, this was picnic time.

After we'd eaten, he aimed grapes at
my mouth. I flung at him the shells of
pomegranates and ran off. He tracked
me down the river-bank. We battled,
melon-rind and apple-core our arms.
'You two!' grandma cried. 'Stop fighting, you'll
tire yourselves to death!' We didn't listen.

> This was late summer, before the snows
> come to Kashmir and end children's games.

Zulfikar Ghose

Novice waiting for the drag-lift at Les Coches

There is nothing posh
About Les Coches:
The man who runs the drag
Has a woolly hat and a fag.
It is not his job to encourage
Only to growl and manage
Unruly poles or people
Who fumble and topple.
He is merciless
To anyone who makes a mess:
Anyone who falls
He calls
Something hard to translate
And they have to wait. And wait.

Shuffle forward. Grab the rail.
(Stab your neighbour with your ski-pole.)
Sorry, mate – my first go:
Hard to stay up on this slippery snow.
Look at that bloke! What control!
I see – like *that* – you grab the pole –
Let it pull you for a bit
Then up and under – and back you sit
Not too far – then you flex your knees
And make sure you don't cross your skis.
I'm getting closer: three to go.
I'm worried about those ruts in the snow!
Too late now – I'm up to the gate:
Ski-poles in the left hand – both skis straight.
Here comes the pole – steady, steady – hold tight!
Pull it through, sit back. There, that's right.
Knees bend – and extend. Keep your skis together.
Keep control. WATCH THAT HOLE! Made it.
    Take a breather.
Right. I've got it. That wasn't so tough.
But how the heck do I get off?

John Hill

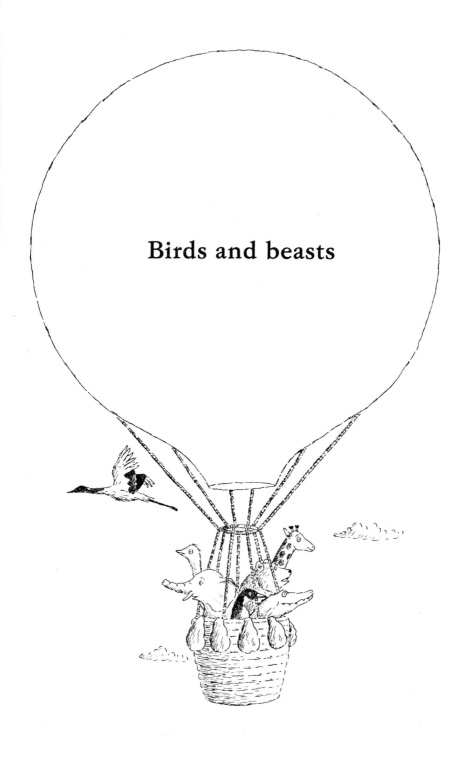

Birds and beasts

The Peruvian llama

An extraordinary beast is the llama.
Almost oval, yet oblong and square,
Not a fish, nor a fowl,
Neither fruit-bat nor owl,
And its coat's not quite wool, not quite hair.

An unusual beast is the llama,
The Peruvians cherish it most:
For they feed it on chocs
And then herd it (in flocks)
From the Andes right down to the coast.

A remarkable beast is the llama,
And its habits are skittish and quaint;
When they shave off its fleece,
The poor llama says: 'Please
Won't you give me a new coat, of paint?'

An impossible beast is the llama,
Like a goat, but with much longer legs;
And a hairy great snout
Which it turns inside out
As it drops to its knees and it begs:

'I'm a sad little beast, I'm a llama;
And it hurts when I'm prodded or poked,
For it truly upsets me
When my master forgets me:
It's a blessing I'm hard to provoke!'

An unfortunate beast is the llama,
Neither elegant, charming, nor cute;
If its life isn't full
As a grower of wool,
Can we ever console the poor brute?

Christopher Mann

Antarctica

For the penguin there's no problem in Antarctica,
As he pecks himself a perch amid the snow,
For the penguin it's a doddle in Antarctica,
As he waddles and he paddles to and fro.

For the seagull life's a breeze in Antarctica,
As she sails and soars and swoops above the ice;
For the seagull likes to freeze in Antarctica,
And she's never found another place so nice.

For the tuna and the pilchard in Antarctica,
There is safety to be found in waters dim;
For they adore the icy oceans of Antarctica,
While in warmer waters hungry hunters swim.

But the humans who adventure in Antarctica,
Must endure the biting winds and freezing rain;
For the weather is appalling in Antarctica,
And a tourist seldom wants to go again!

Christopher Mann

The ostrich

The ostrich roams the great Sahara,
Its mouth is wide, its neck is narra.
It has such long and lofty legs,
I'm glad it sits to lay its eggs.

Ogden Nash

Ibis

The Ibis is a sacred Bird
    and lives beside the Nile.
She looks just like the letter S
And eats the eggs – with watercress –
    of the great Crocodile.

The Ibis is a sacred Bird:
    her neck is long and black.
If taken from the River Nile
She dies in a little while
    of pining to go back.

George Barker

48

The Afghan Hound

The Afghan Hound
Is seldom found
On high Himalayan plains;
He lives instead
In a wicker bed
In a terraced house in Staines.

He goes for walks
In Bucks and Yorks
In search of doggy thrills;
In his shaggy coat
He's like a goat
But he never climbs the hills.

He's tall and slim,
And full of vim,
And smarter than Chow or Peke:
Unthinkable
To risk Kabul
And Russian hide-and-seek.

He might have been
A mujaheddin,
And in ambush lie in wait;
Or patrol around
An Afghan town
As a watchdog for the state.

But here he sleeps,
And never weeps
For the mountains far away;
For the Afghan Hound
Prefers low ground,
And three square meals a day.

Christopher Mann

49

The flower-fed buffaloes

The flower-fed buffaloes of the spring
In the days of long ago,
Ranged where the locomotives sing
And the prairie flowers lie low:—
The tossing, blooming, perfumed grass
Is swept away by the wheat,
Wheels and wheels and wheels spin by
In the spring that still is sweet.
But the flower-fed buffaloes of the spring
Left us, long ago.
They gore no more, they bellow no more,
They trundle around the hills no more:—
With the Blackfeet, lying low,
With the Pawnees, lying low,
Lying low.

Vachel Lindsay

50

Nairobi National Park

Ostrich and giraffe peek
Over bush; warthog and
Baboon amble across roads;
From lone tree to Songora
Ridge drift the heifers,
But shy in the grass
The lion lies,
And placid are the ponds
In Embakasi Plain.

John Pepper Clark

Greek fishcats

Three white cats,
spring kittens taught by summer,
advance from three directions;

slink down steps
so white they only show in shade
where autumn sun should hide them;

slide round boxes
rubbing smells from fishy nets
to show each other;

pounce and purr
untangling upright tails,
enjoy the morning prospects.

Painted boats
at rest inside the harbour
slap their own reflections

waiting. Fishermen
depart for liquid breakfasts.
Then the cats board, bolder.

Stout mothers come
to coil wet ropes or spread
the yellow, pink edged nets

and stay to batter
octopus to death on rocks
until the flesh is tender.

Small fry scatter,
fins and tails shed
silvery scales, subsiding.

Work is finished.
Shadows let out cats
to clean up this new morning.

Jane Whittle

The Barrier Reef

The Barrier Reef is a coral puzzle
Whose future is in the question
Because of the starfish who gobble and guzzle
And never get indigestion.
Reporters asked them why they ate
At such a rapid, rabid rate.
In between bites the coral harriers
Said, 'It's just that we don't like barriers'.

Marguerite Varday

The starling

The starling is my darling, although
I don't much approve of its
Habits. Proletarian bird,
Nesting in holes and corners, making a mess,
And sometimes dropping its eggs
Just any old where – on the front lawn, for
    instance.

It thinks it can sing too. In springtime
They are on every rooftop, or high bough,
Or telegraph pole, blithering away
Discords, with clichés picked up
From the other melodists.

But go to Trafalgar Square,
And stand, about sundown, on the steps of St
    Martin's;
Mark then, in the air,
The starlings, before they roost, at their evolutions –
Scores of starlings, wheeling,
Steaming and twisting, the whole murmuration
Turning like one bird: an image
Realized, of the City.

    John Heath-Stubbs

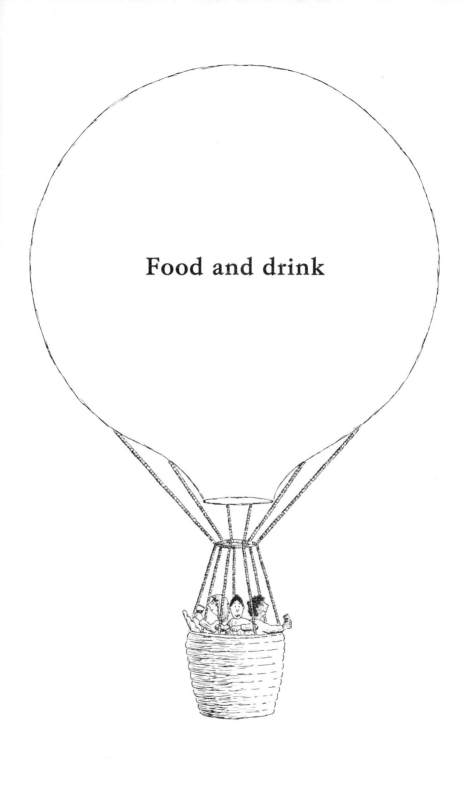

Food and drink

On Nevski Bridge

On Nevski Bridge a Russian stood
Chewing his beard for lack of food.
Said he, 'This stuff is tough to eat
But a darn sight better than shredded wheat.'

Anon

Chop-suey

There was a man who in the East
Made sweet-sour soups, a Chinese feast
Of birds' nests, sharks' fins, pancake rolls,
And piles of rice with shrimps in bowls.

In many cities in the West
This man built cafés. Every guest
Was given plastic chopsticks and
A finger-bowl to wash each hand.

The menu written out was good
And many people liked the food.
The dishes offered pleased the young,
And *no one* jested, 'Who flung dung?'

Now every town and every street
Serves pancake rolls, pork sour and sweet,
And yet amongst the bamboo-shoots
We taste old hot-pots, chips, and sprouts.

Elizabeth Jennings

Fiesta melons

In Benidorm there are melons,
Whole donkey-carts full

Of innumerable melons,
Ovals and balls,

Bright and green and thumpable
Laced over with stripes

Of turtle-dark green.
Choose an egg-shape, a world-shape,

Bowl one homeward to taste
In the whitehot noon.

Cream-smooth honeydews,
Pink-pulped whoppers,

Bump-rinded cantaloupes
With orange cores.

Sylvia Plath

57

Mango, little Mango

The Mango stands for Africa
  in its taste
  in its smell
  in its colour
  in its shape.

The Mango has the shape of a heart –
  Africa too!
It has a taste that's hot, strong and sweet –
  Africa too!
It has a reddy-brown shade
  like the tanned plains
  of my beloved earth.
Because of this I love you and your taste
  Mango!
Heart of fruit, sweet and mild.

You are the love of Africa
  because beating in your breast
  is Africa's heart,
Oh Mango, little Mango,
  love of Africa!

    Anon
    Translated by Chris Searle

An explorer named Mortimer Craft

An explorer named Mortimer Craft
While in Africa ate spiced giraffe.
The effect of this food
Was a sound deep and rude
And green flames that shot out fore and aft.

Mick Gowar

Craster kippers

Three Craster fishermen set out one day,
To cast their nets beyond the bay,
But alas for Aidan and Andrew and Tim,
Those nets were moth-eaten, their holes wearing
    thin!
So they lost fifty cod-fish and twenty-two trout.
Says Aidan, 'Lord save us, they're all slipping out!'
They caught fifty herring, but twelve got away.
Says Andrew, 'At this rate we'll ne'er earn our pay!'
But they caught seventy mackerel, of flounders a
    score,
Two dace, and of whiting a dozen or more.
Now tell me, if you can, I pray,
Of all the fish they caught that day,
How many kippers got away?

They sell fresh kippers by the strand,
At Craster in Northumberland,
And it's 'Kippers! Fresh Kippers! Fresh Kippers!'
    all day,
But how many kippers got away?

John Cunliffe

Song of the aborigines of Arnhem Land, Australia

The prawn is there, at the place of the Dugong,
    digging mud with its claws . . .
The hard-shelled prawn, living there in the water,
    making soft little noises.
It burrows into the mud and casts it aside among
    the lilies . . .
Throwing aside the mud with soft little noises . . .
Digging out mud with its claws at the place of the
    Dugong, the place of the Dugong's bed . . .
The prawn is burrowing, coming up, throwing
    aside the mud, and digging,
Climbing up to the lotus plants and up to their
    pools.

Traditional

Mad Dogs and Englishmen

(with apologies to Noël Coward)

Mad Dogs and Englishmen
Have Prawn Vindaloo for lunch;
The Ceylonese don't care to,
The Goanese don't dare to,
In Katmandu
They simply chew
On a bar of 'Harvest Crunch';
But Mad Dogs and Englishmen
Have Prawn Vindaloo for lunch!

Mad Dogs and Englishmen
Have Tandoori Lamb for tea;
The Pakistanis hate it,
The Sikhs won't contemplate it,
In the Khyber Pass
They drink a glass
Of ice-cold G and T,
But Mad Dogs and Englishmen
Have Tandoori Lamb for tea!

Mad Dogs and Englishmen
Have curry for breakfast too,
Bengali folk have banned it,
Pathans can't understand it,
In Hyderabad
They think it's sad
That the Brits have gone cuckoo –
But Mad Dogs and Englishmen
Have curry for lunch
And curry for brunch
And curry for breakfast too!

Christopher Mann

Jamaica market

Honey, pepper, leaf-green limes,
Pagan fruit whose names are rhymes,
Mangoes, breadfruit, ginger-roots,
Granadillas, bamboo-shoots,
Cho-cho, ackees, tangerines,
Lemons, purple Congo-beans,
Sugar, okras, kola-nuts,
Citrons, hairy coconuts,
Fish, tobacco, native hats,
Gold bananas, woven mats,
Plantains, wild thyme, pallid leeks,
Pigeons with their scarlet beaks,
Oranges and saffron yams,
Baskets, ruby guava jams,
Turtles, goat-skins, cinnamon,
Allspice, conch-shells, golden rum.
Black skins, babel – and the sun
That burns all colours into one.

Agnes Maxwell-Hall

Holidays at home

There was a family who, every year,
Would go abroad, sometimes to Italy,
Sometimes to France. The youngest did not dare
To say, 'I much prefer to stay right here.'

You see, abroad there were no slot-machines,
No bright pink rock with one name going through
    it,
No rain, no boarding-houses, no baked beans,
No landladies, and no familiar scenes.

And George, the youngest boy, so longed to say,
'I don't *like* Greece. I don't like all these views,
I don't like having fierce sun every day,
And, most of all, I just detest the way

The food is cooked – that garlic and that soup,
Those strings of pasta, and no cakes at all.'
The family wondered why George seemed to droop
And looked just like a thin hen in a coop.

They never guessed why when they said, 'Next year
We can't afford abroad, we'll stay right here,'
George looked so pleased and soon began to
    dream
Of piers, pink rock, deep sand, and Devonshire
    cream.

Elizabeth Jennings

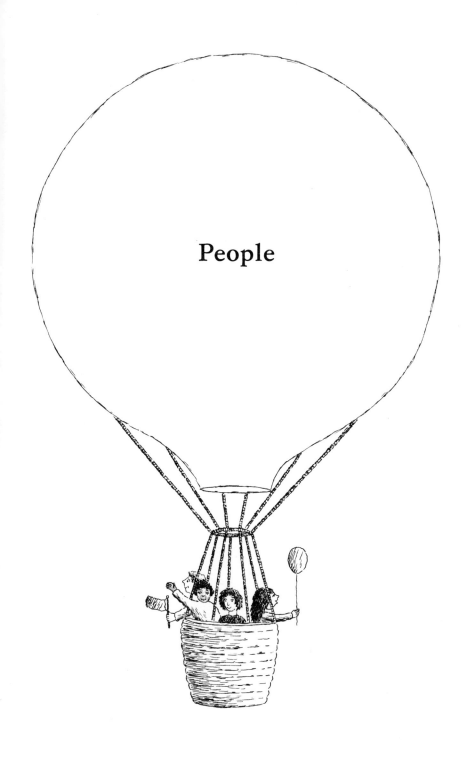

People

The negro speaks of rivers

I've known rivers:
I've known rivers ancient as the world and older
than the flow of human blood in human veins.

My soul has grown deep like the rivers.

I bathed in the Euphrates when dawns were young,
I built my hut near the Congo and it lulled me to
sleep.
I looked upon the Nile and raised the pyramids
above it.
I heard the singing of the Mississippi when Abe
Lincoln went down to New Orleans, and I've
seen its muddy bosom turn all golden in the
sunset.

I've known rivers:
Ancient, dusky rivers.

My soul has grown deep like the rivers.

Langston Hughes

The donkey boys

I pass them on the seashore early,
Two Spanish boys in the sun. One ten,
The other six. They wave and smile at me,
Then bend their ragged backs again

To search the driftwood and sort out
Light dry sticks for bedding. Their donkey
Is small and white. He stands there without
Moving. His eyes and ears are sleepy.

The panniers that they must heap
Up high are huge. They work steadily,
Smiling as they go. As if asleep,
Their donkey follows quietly.

One morning I met them riding
Past the school where children were at play.
The boys didn't look at them, but smiling
Went on gently to their work that day.

Albert Rowe

Plucking the rushes

A boy and girl are sent to gather rushes for thatching.
(Fourth or fifth century)

Green rushes with red shoots,
Long leaves bending to the wind –
You and I in the same boat
Plucking rushes at the Five Lakes.
We started at dawn from the orchid-island;
We rested under the elms till noon.
You and I plucking rushes
Had not plucked a handful when night came!

Anon
Translated from the Chinese by Arthur Waley

There was a young lady of Niger

There was a young lady of Niger
Who smiled as she rode on a Tiger;
   They came back from the ride
   With the lady inside,
And the smile on the face of the Tiger.

Anon

Siberia

Deep in the Arctic Circle
Where the wild, wild winds roar,
The night lasts all day long,
And in the murk the hungry lupines howl.
Across the endless plains
The eternal wastes of Siberia far into Mongolia.
Natives cling to the earth
Hardened by unchanging frost
And hollow in their hovels,
They wrap their sheepskins
Round their bodies, skin upon skin to keep at bay
The bitter frost,
A tough breed of men, they are accustomed to cold
    comfort
and twilight life.
And overhead the stars look down and mirror
The distant ice, as howls the wind
And whines the fox, far from the crowds of city life
    and light.

Lucretia King (11)

My auntie

My auntie who lives in
Llanfairpwllgwyngyllgogerych-
    wyrndrobwllllantysiliogogogoch
Has asked me to stay.

But unfortunately
Llanfairpwllgwyngyllgogerych-
    wyrndrobwllllantysiliogogogoch
Is a long, long way away.

Will I ever go to
Llanfairpwllgwyngyllgogerych-
    wyrndrobwllllantysiliogogogoch?
It's difficult to say.

Colin West

Llook you!

Once in Wales
We saw
A frogogogogoch
Lleaping ofor
A llogogogogoch!

Geoffrey Summerfield

70

My grandfather in Cyprus

I'd like to meet my grandad
But he lives in a land far away,
Where it is hot and sunny.
I hear he is an old man now,
His face is wrinkled like a lemon in the sun.
When we meet
We will talk in Greek
Someday.

Michael Xenofontos

A grand obsession
For Rosemary Lee

Grandma said, with a nod of her head,
'As sure as one and one make two,
I'll go and see the Grand Canyon
If it's the last thing I do!'

So every day for years
She saved all her cash,
Sometimes frowned and shook her head:
'I think I'm being very rash.'

Once a month she wondered,
But that grand hole in the ground
Sat tight inside her head
All the year round.

Finally she'd saved enough
And went and paid her fare.
Put piles of cash on the counter,
And said, 'Now I'll soon be there!'

71

Slowly she packed her bags.
'Shall I take this coat or that?
Does it ever rain in Arizona?
Shall I need to take a hat?'

A Jumbo took her to Los Angeles,
An elephant with wings;
She saw millions of cars like performing fleas
Going round and round in rings.

She went to look at the film stars' homes,
To peep and poke her nose.
But all she saw was fences and walls
And a gardener with a hose.

Then round Las Vegas's neon streets
She took a daring ramble,
Saw elastic acrobats cabaret
And decided not to gamble.

Then she took the coach to the Canyon,
Her eyes nearly popped out of her head.
The sunset glowed on redstone cliffs.
'It's even better than they said!'

Next morning, bright and early,
Almost before first light,
She went to the local airfield
And asked to take a flight.

A young pilot said he'd take her
And show her all the sights.
'But your plane's so very small!' she said.
'Is it big enough for flights?'

The pilot held up his finger.
'The wind's not too strong,' he said.
So they clambered aboard and took off,
And she thought, 'I'll soon be dead.'

He flew straight into the Canyon,
And tipped the plane on its side.
'You've never seen anything like this!' he said.
'Are you enjoying the ride?'

Her stomach went quite crazy.
The blood rushed to her head.
Her vision went blurred and hazy.
'It's very interesting,' she said.

Soon she got used to the flying,
And sat back snug in her seat.
Saw great rocks, and the river winding
Like a ribbon beneath her feet. . . .

A week later we met her at the airport,
Safe and sound, back on land.
'How'd you like the Grand Canyon?' we asked her.
'The Grand Canyon? Oh, it was grand!'

                    Geoffrey Summerfield

Alabama

My brethren,
among the legends of my people
it is told how a chief,
leading the remnant of his people,
crossed a great river,
and striking his tipi-stake upon the ground,
exclaimed, 'A-la-ba-ma!'
This in our language means
'Here we may rest!'
But he saw not the future.
The white man came:
he and his people could not rest there;
they were driven out,
and in a dark swamp
they were thrust down into the slime
and killed.
The word he so sadly spoke
has given a name to one of the white man's states.
There is no spot under those stars
that now smile upon us,
where the Indian can plant his foot
and sigh 'A-la-ba-ma.'

Khe-tha-a-hi (Eagle Wing)

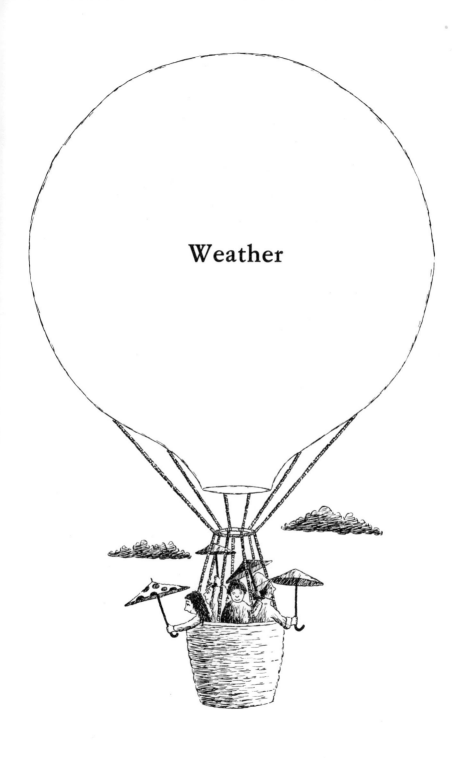

Weather

Rain song of the North American Indians

Hi-iya, naiho-o! The earth is rumbling
From the beating of our basket drums.
The earth is rumbling from the beating
Of our basket drums, everywhere humming.
Earth is rumbling, everywhere raining.

Hi-iya, naiho-o! Pluck out the feathers
    From the wing of the eagle and turn them
Toward the east where lie the large clouds.
    Hi-iya, naiho-o! Pluck out the soft down
From the breast of the eagle and turn it
    Toward the west where sail the small clouds.
Hi-iya, naiho-o! Beneath the abode
    Of the rain gods it is thundering;
Large corn is there. *Hi-iya, naiho-o!*
    Beneath the abode of the rain gods
It is raining; small corn is there.

Traditional

Watch your step, I'm drenched

In Manchester there are a thousand puddles.
Bus-queue puddles poised on slanting paving
    stones,
Railway puddles slouching outside stations,
Cinema puddles in ambush at the exits,
Zebra-crossing puddles in dips of the dark stripes –
They lurk in the murk
Of the north-western evening
For the sake of their notorious joke,
Their only joke – to soak
The tights or trousers of the citizens.
Each splash and consequent curse is echoed by
One thousand dark Mancunian puddle chuckles.

In Manchester there lives the King of Puddles,
Master of Miniature Muck Lakes,
The Shah of Slosh, Splendifero of Splash,
Prince, Pasha and Pope of Puddledom.
Where? Somewhere. The rain-headed ruler
Lies doggo, incognito,
Disguised as an average, accidental mini-pool.
He is scared as any other emperor,
For one night, all his soiled and soggy victims
Might storm his streets, assassination in their
    minds,
A thousand rolls of blotting paper in their hands,
And drink his shadowed, one-joke life away.

Adrian Mitchell

The Umbrella bird

The Umbrella bird is known to live
In Ecuador and Peru,
With several aunts and uncles
In Brazil and Chile too.

If often rains in those parts,
Which suits them without doubt
For unless it's raining quite a lot
Umbrella birds won't come out.

Martin Honeysett

Albatross

Hush. . .hush. . .hush. . .
The grey wind comes with a rush,
The cold wind comes with a wail,
And gliding across
The gale full sail
Lo! the Albatross.
The wind is her father,
The sea her mother,
She was born in a lather
Of foam and a smother
Of snow, long ago,
Before the ice was old.
She is careless and calm, and as cold
As a fleece of snow,
She is lovely and large, and as lone
As the Arctic Zone.
The wind
And the sea
Between them toss
Their daughter, the Albatross.

Eleanor Farjeon

The Ice King

Where the world is grey and lone
Sits the Ice King on his throne –

Passionless, austere, afar,
Underneath the Polar Star.

Over all his splendid plains
An eternal stillness reigns.

Silent creatures of the North,
White and strange and fierce, steal forth:

Soft-foot beasts from frozen lair,
Noiseless birds that wing the air,

Souls of seamen dead, who lie
Stark beneath the pale north sky;

Shapes to living eye unknown,
Wild and shy, come round the throne

Where the Ice King sits in view
To receive their homage due.

But the Ice King's quiet eyes,
Calm, implacable, and wise,

Gaze beyond the silent throng,
With a steadfast look and long,

Down to where the summer streams
Murmur in their golden dreams,

Where the sky is rich and deep,
Where warm stars bring down warm sleep,

Where the days are, every one,
Clad with warmth and crowned with sun.

And the longing gods may feel
Stirs within his heart of steel,

And he yearns far forth to go
From his land of ice and snow.

But forever, grey and lone,
Sits the Ice King on his throne –

Passionless, austere, afar,
Underneath the Polar Star.

A. B. Demille

Trade Winds

In the harbour, in the island, in the Spanish Seas,
Are the tiny white houses and the orange-trees,
And day-long, night-long, the cool and pleasant
    breeze
    Of the steady Trade Winds blowing.

There is the red wine, the nutty Spanish ale,
The shuffle of the dancers, the old salt's tale,
The squeaking fiddle, and the soughing in the sail
    Of the steady Trade Winds blowing.

And o'nights there's fire-flies and the yellow moon,
And in the ghostly palm-trees the sleepy tune
Of the quiet voice calling me, the long low croon
    Of the steady Trade Winds blowing.

John Masefield

82

Nature

We have neither Summer nor Winter,
Neither Autumn nor Spring.

We have instead the days
When gold sun shines on the lush green cane fields
Magnificently.

The days when the rain beats like bullets on the
    roofs
And there is no sound but the swish of water in the
    gullies
And trees struggling in the high Jamaica winds.

Also there are the days when the leaves fade from
    off guango trees
And the reaped cornfields lie bare and fallow in the
    sun.

But best of all there are the days when the mango
    and the logwood blossom

When the bushes are full of the sound of bees and
    the scent of honey,
When the tall grass sways and shivers to the
    slightest breath of air,

When the buttercups have paved the earth with
    yellow stars,
And beauty comes suddenly and the rains have
    gone.

H. D. Carberry

Marigolds in Morocco

They walk among the marigolds
In Morocco, in the Spring,
Like swimmers in a sea of suns
Beneath a sun-drenched sky.
And they picnic in the marigolds
On a cloth of orange haze,
On Sundays in Morocco –
Sweet shining golden days.

Jenny Craig

An Irish washday

A sky like dirty dishwater
Is slopped above the earth,
It washes out a foam of cloud
Towards the bleary sun

From peat bogs mountains raise their heads
To cough out puffs of mist,
The ocean rocks two little boats
Upon her huge green hip

And rain is dribbled thickly down,
Spat from the grubby clouds,
To mix the mud and stain the stones
And keep the people in

The washing only, on the line,
Is left out to the rain,
It flies out on the filthy wind,
While bravely suffering

Emma Payne

Evening: Ponte al Mare, Pisa

The sun is set; the swallows are asleep;
  The bats are flitting fast in the grey air;
The slow soft toads out of damp corners creep,
  And evening's breath, wandering here and there
Over the quivering surface of the stream,
Wakes not one ripple from its summer dream.

There is no dew on the dry grass tonight,
  Nor damp within the shadow of the trees;
The wind is intermitting, dry, and light;
  And in the inconstant motion of the breeze
The dust and straws are driven up and down,
And whirled about the pavement of the town.

Within the surface of the fleeting river
  The wrinkled image of the city lay,
Immovably unquiet, and for ever
  It trembles, but it never fades away. . .

Percy Bysshe Shelley

The tough guy of London

Seen from within a heated room,
On a sunny February afternoon,
London looks like
Any other summer's day.

Step out in only
Your shirt and trousers
And, even with a black belt in karate,
An invisible tough guy
With blimey cold hands and feet,
Punches you
Smack on the nose
Straight back in.

Kojo Gyinawe Kyei

Greek noon

Heat hangs like a curtain,
Shimmers on the polished rocks
And veils the distant olive green
Like a potter's glaze.

In the dusty road a chicken struts,
Pecks, pauses,
Paces back
Into splashed-ink shadows.

Whitewashed houses glare at empty streets,
Silent as tombs,
Stoutly concealing
Their shuttered inhabitants.

By the church of Holy Wisdom
A priest quickly passes,
Crow-stepping with a flap of robe
Across the glowing courtyard.

In a wooden corner of the taverna
Sits the victor of 1940,
Eyes wet with memories,
Chin grey-stubbled by the long defeat.

And the waiter serves kebabs
To tourists from another time-zone,
While the village hides its face
From the wrath of the sun.

Christopher Mann

Quickstep

Way down Geneva,
All along Vine,
Deeper than the snowdrift
Love's eyes shine:

Mary Lou's walking
In the winter time.

She's got

Red boots on, she's got
Red boots on,
Kicking up the winter
Till the winter's gone.

So

Go by Ontario,
Look down Main,
If you can't Mary Lou
Come back again:

Sweet light burning
In winter's flame.

She's got

Snow in her eyes, got
A tingle in her toes
And new red boots on
Wherever she goes.

So

All around Lake Street,
Up by St Paul,
Quicker than the white wind
Love takes all:

Mary Lou's walking
In the big snow fall.

She's got

Red boots on, she's got
Red boots on,
Kicking up the winter
Till the winter's gone.

Kit Wright

P.S.

The Human Race

The Swiss are clean, the Scots are mean,
The French have a charm that pleases,
Germans like work, but Mexicans shirk,
The Dutch grow bulbs and cheeses.

The Russians are given to dance on their knees,
Americans crave apple pie,
In Iceland they just sit and freeze,
In Gambia, they fry.

Italians thrive on pasta and wine,
The Eskimoes rub noses,
The Welsh can sing like a heavenly choir,
But Englishmen grow roses.

They put us all in boxes,
And label us by place.
The truth is, we live separate lives,
But we're all in The Human Race.

Jenny Craig

Index of first lines

Index of authors

Acknowledgements

The editors and publishers would like to thank the following for permission to use copyright material in this collection. The publishers have made every effort to contact the copyright holders but there are a few cases where it has not been possible to do so. We would be grateful to hear from anyone who can enable us to contact them so the omission can be corrected at the first opportunity.

Angus & Robertson (UK) Ltd for 'The fastest train in the world' by Keith Bosley from *And I Dance*.
Benjamin Bolt for 'Boules'.
Cadbury Ltd for 'Siberia' by Lucretia King from *Cadbury's Third Book of Children's Poetry* published in conjunction with the Cadbury National Exhibition of Children's Art.
Century Hutchinson Ltd for 'My auntie' by Colin West from *It's Funny When You Look At It*.
Constable Publishers for 'Plucking at the rushes' translated by Arthur Walley from *170 Chinese Poems*.
Curtis Brown Ltd for 'The whales off Wales' by X.J. Kennedy from *One Winter Night in August* (Atheneum) © X.J. Kennedy.
Andre Deutsch for 'Llook you' and 'A grand obses-

sion' by Geoffrey Summerfield from *Welcome* and
'Craster kippers' by John Cunliffe from *Riddles
Rhymes and Rigmaroles*.

Reprinted by permission of Faber and Faber Ltd 'Ibis'
from *The Alphabetical Zoo* by George Baker.

Roy Fuller as author for 'Australia' from *Seen Grandpa
Lately?* (Andre Deutsch).

Mick Gowar for 'An explorer named Mortimer Craft'
from *What a Lot of Nonsense* (Robert Royce).

David Higham Associates Ltd for 'The starling' by
John Heath Stubbs; 'Albatross' by Eleanor Farjeon
from *Silver Sand and Snow*; 'Tarragon, tansy, thyme
and teasel' and 'Victoria' by Eleanor Farjeon from
Puffin Quartet (Penguin); 'Chop-suey' and 'Holidays
at home' by Elizabeth Jennings from *Poets in Hand*
(Puffin); 'May music in Castille' by Ted Walker
from *Over the Bridge* (Kestrel).

John Hill for 'Novice waiting for the drag-lift at Les
Coches', 'The last steam train to Margate' and
'Rickshaw ride'.

Olwyn Hughes for 'Fiesta melons' by Sylvia Plath
from *Collected Poems 1981* published Faber & Faber
Ltd © Ted Hughes 1981.

Barbara Ireson for 'Night train to Istanbul' by A.
Elliot-Cannon and 'The subway in New York' by
Tsutoma Fukuda both from *Moving Along* (Evans
Brothers).

'The negro speaks of rivers' Copyright 1926 by Alfred
A. Knopf, Inc. and renewed 1954 by Langston
Hughes. Reprinted from *Selected Poems of Langston
Hughes* by permission of Alfred A. Knopf, Inc.

Kojo Gyinaye Kyei for 'The tough guy of London'
from *Is a Caterpillar Ticklish?* (Robert Royce).

Christopher Mann for 'The Peruvian llama', 'Antarctic',
'The Afghan Hound', 'Mad Dogs and Englishmen'
and 'Greek noon'.

Methuen Children's Books for 'The Umbrella bird' by
Martin Honeysett from *Animal Nonsense Rhymes*.

Adrian Mitchell for 'Watch your step, I'm drenched'
from *The Apeman Cometh* (Jonathan Cape).

Reprinted by permission of Oxford University Press

'Limbo' © Edward Kamau Braithwaite 1973 from *The Arrivants* by Edward Kamau Braithwaite (1973).

Emma Payne for 'An Irish washday'.

Penguin Books Australia Ltd for 'My auntie from Spain' by Doug Macleod from *The Fed Up Family Album* (Kestrel).

Reproduced by permission of Penguin Books Ltd 'The traveller' from *Late Home* (Kestrel Books, 1976), copyright © Brian Lee, 1976, pp 32–3; 'The Ostrich' and 'Russian dance' from *Custard and Company* by Ogden Nash, selected and illustrated by Quentin Blake (Kestrel Books, 1979), copyright © 1979 by the Estate of Ogden Nash, this selection copyright © Quentin Blake 1979, pp. 31, 107.

Reprinted by permission of the James Reeves Estate 'If Pigs could fly' by James Reeves © James Reeves Estate.

Albert Rowe for 'The donkey boys' from *A Second Poetry Book* (Oxford University Press).

The Society of Authors as the literary representative of the Estate of Rose Fyleman for 'Three French mice' translated by Rose Fyleman.

Jane Whittle for 'Greek fishcats', 'Crossing Ireland by train' and 'A post card from Greece'.

Ian Whybrow for 'The sleeptrotting globewisher', 'How a car-journey etc' and 'France at a glance'.

Young World Books for 'My grandfather in Cyprus' by Michael Xenofontos from *Our City*.